Ha

by Bill Fyfe Hendrie

Lang**Syne**
PUBLISHING
WRITING *to* REMEMBER

Lang**Syne**

PUBLISHING

WRITING *to* REMEMBER

79 Main Street, Newtongrange,
Midlothian EH22 4NA
Tel: 0131 344 0414   Fax: 0845 075 6085
E-mail: info@lang-syne.co.uk
www.langsyneshop.co.uk

Design by Dorothy Meikle
Printed by Ricoh Print Scotland
© Lang Syne Publishers Ltd 2014

ISBN 978-1-85217-067-7

Hamilton

SEPT NAMES INCLUDE:
Abercorn
Alexander
Brownlee
Cadzow
Leeper
Leipers
Preston
Selkirk

Hamilton

MOTTO:
Through.

CREST:
An Oak Tree Penetrated
by a Frame Saw.

TERRITORY:
Renfrewshire and Lanarkshire.

Chapter one:

The origins of the clan system

by Rennie McOwan

The original Scottish clans of the Highlands and the great families of the Lowlands and Borders were gatherings of families, relatives, allies and neighbours for mutual protection against rivals or invaders.

Scotland experienced invasion from the Vikings, the Romans and English armies from the south. The Norman invasion of what is now England also had an influence on land-holding in Scotland. Some of these invaders stayed on and in time became 'Scottish'.

The word clan derives from the Gaelic language term 'clann', meaning children, and it was first used many centuries ago as communities were formed around tribal lands in glens and mountain fastnesses.

The format of clans changed over the centuries, but at its best the chief and his family held the land on behalf of all, like trustees, and the ordinary clansmen and women believed they had a blood relationship with the founder of their clan.

There were two way duties and obligations. An inadequate chief could be deposed and replaced by someone of greater ability.

Clan people had an immense pride in race. Their relationship with the chief was like adult children to a father and they had a real dignity.

The concept of clanship is very old and a more feudal notion of authority gradually crept in.

Pictland, for instance, was divided into seven principalities ruled by feudal leaders who were the strongest and most charismatic leaders of their particular groups.

By the sixth century the 'British' kingdoms of Strathclyde, Lothian and Celtic Dalriada (Argyll) had emerged and Scotland, as one nation, began to take shape in the time of King Kenneth MacAlpin.

Some chiefs claimed descent from

ancient kings which may not have been accurate in every case.

By the twelfth and thirteenth centuries the clans and families were more strongly brought under the central control of Scottish monarchs.

Lands were awarded and administered more and more under royal favour, yet the power of the area clan chiefs was still very great.

The long wars to ensure Scotland's independence against the expansionist ideas of English monarchs extended the influence of some clans and reduced the lands of others.

Those who supported Scotland's greatest king, Robert the Bruce, were awarded the territories of the families who had opposed his claim to the Scottish throne.

In the Scottish Borders country – the notorious Debatable Lands – the great families built up a ferocious reputation for providing warlike men accustomed to raiding into England and occasionally fighting one another.

Chiefs had the power to dispense justice and to confiscate lands and clan warfare produced a society where martial virtues – courage, hardiness, tenacity – were greatly admired.

Gradually the relationship between the clans and the Crown became strained as Scottish monarchs became more orientated to life in the Lowlands and, on occasion, towards England.

The Highland clans spoke a different language, Gaelic, whereas the language of Lowland Scotland and the court was Scots and in more modern times, English.

Highlanders dressed differently, had different customs, and their wild mountain land sometimes seemed almost foreign to people living in the Lowlands.

It must be emphasised that Gaelic culture was very rich and story-telling, poetry, piping, the clarsach (harp) and other music all flourished and were greatly respected.

Highland culture was different from other parts of Scotland but it was not inferior or less sophisticated.

Central Government, whether in London or Edinburgh, sometimes saw the Gaelic clans as

"The spirit of the clan means much to thousands of people"

a challenge to their authority and some sent expeditions into the Highlands and west to crush the power of the Lords of the Isles.

Nevertheless, when the eighteenth century Jacobite Risings came along the cause of the Stuarts was mainly supported by Highland clans.

The word Jacobite comes from the Latin for James – Jacobus. The Jacobites wanted to restore the exiled Stuarts to the throne of Britain.

The monarchies of Scotland and England became one in 1603 when King James VI of Scotland (1st of England) gained the English throne after Queen Elizabeth died.

The Union of Parliaments of Scotland and England, the Treaty of Union, took place in 1707.

Some Highland clans, of course, and Lowland families opposed the Jacobites and supported the incoming Hanoverians.

After the Jacobite cause finally went down at Culloden in 1746 a kind of ethnic cleansing took place. The power of the chiefs was curtailed. Tartan and the pipes were banned in law.

Many emigrated, some because they

wanted to, some because they were evicted by force. In addition, many Highlanders left for the cities of the south to seek work.

Many of the clan lands became home to sheep and deer shooting estates.

But the warlike traditions of the clans and the great Lowland and Border families lived on, with their descendants fighting bravely for freedom in two world wars.

Remember the men from whence you came, says the Gaelic proverb, and to that could be added the role of many heroic women.

The spirit of the clan, of having roots, whether Highland or Lowland, means much to thousands of people.

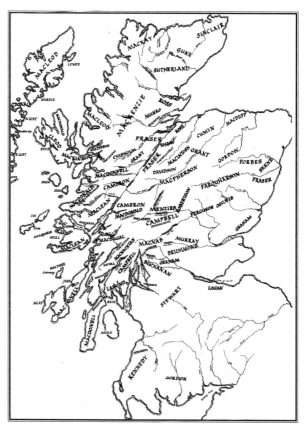

A map of the clans' homelands

Chapter two:

"For true service and great manhood"

"For true service and great manhood in slaying the General Lieutenant of England upon Kinneil Muir, King Robert gave all the lands of Kinneil to Sir Gilbert Hamilton."

Thus according to the monk, Friar Mark, in the earliest written history of the House of Hamilton did the family acquire the estate high above the Forth from which the ruins of the Palace of Kinneil still command magnificent views across the river to the shores of Fife and the Ochil Hills beyond.

At the same time that Sir Gilbert received Kinneil, his religious biographer, Friar Mark, also notes that the grateful King Robert the Bruce granted the Hamiltons their coat of arms of "three cinqufois on a bloody ground".

While The Bruce had good reason to be

grateful to Hamilton because in addition to his brave exploits on Kinneil Muir, he was also one of the seven Scottish knights who formed the Royal bodyguard at the Battle of Bannockburn in 1314, another version of how the Hamiltons gained their lands insists that they were actually not granted until 1323 and then not to Gilbert but to his son Walter, who had defended Bothwell Castle for the English and not switched allegiance to the Scottish side until after its fall.

No matter, however, how the Hamiltons came by Kinneil in the midst of the ever changing swirl of Scottish political manoeuverings of the 14th century, they do appear to have been definitely in royal favour by the time of the Bruce's death in 1329. For it was Hamilton senior who was chosen to give the oration at the burial of the King's body in Dunfermline Abbey.

To strengthen their hold on their lands of Kinneil, midway between Bo'ness and Grangemouth, the Hamiltons soon built a tall, thick, stone-walled peel tower high above the rocky ravine of the Gil Burn where it crashes down the hillside to join the River Forth. This was an excellent defensive site and parts of the ancient fortification with its narrow arrow-slit windows and gun-ports still dominate the scene above the burn.

At around the same time, the Hamiltons also were awarded lands in Lanarkshire where they built Castle Cadzow just to the south of Hamilton, the town which grew up nearby and bears the family name. The next of the family to play a prominent part in Scottish affairs of state was James Cadzow who became the first Lord Hamilton in 1445.

Linked through marriage to the Douglas family, the new Lord Hamilton supported them against King James II when royal troops besieged their castle at Abercorn, between Bo'ness and Queensferry, in 1455. Despite mustering a strong force of men, they were unsuccessful in raising the royal siege. A few months later King James also succeeded in capturing the other Douglas stronghold, Inveravon Castle, three miles to the west of the Hamiltons' seat at Kinneil.

Before Kinneil incurred equal royal disfavour, the Hamiltons switched sides and in October of the same year received a special charter from the king, guaranteeing their future rights to all of their lands both at Kinneil and Hamilton.

Lord James also extended his lands in novel fashion. He pioneered land reclamation in Scotland by building a dam across Kinneil Bay and slowly winning valuable acres across from the River Forth. It took seven years to rid the new fields of salt, but by the 1470s they were fit to be farmed and in 1474, the year of his second marriage to Princess Mary, sister of King James III, his new brother-in-law saw fit to confirm the rights to the new lands to the happy pair. In turn they granted the rents from them to support a new church and hospital which they built on the high ground roughly midway between Kinneil and Hamilton at Shotts in Lanarkshire.

Lord Hamilton's second wife, Mary Stewart, was formerly married to the Earl of Arran and when his young son James succeeded him in 1479, that title was subsequently conferred upon

him at a ceremony at Holyrood Palace when he
visited Edinburgh in 1503 to attend the wedding
of his cousin King James IV to the 14-year-old
English Princess Margaret at the marriage of The
Thistle and The Rose as it became romantically
entitled. It was stated that the lands and Earldom
of Arran were bestowed upon him in recognition
of, "his nearness of blood, his services and spe-
cially for his labours and expenses at the time of
the royal marriage".

The second Lord James, Earl of Arran,
had the reputation of being the best archer on foot
or on horse in the whole of Scotland and kept a
famous stud of horses at Kinneil where King
James IV paid a royal visit to the stables in 1508.

With Scotland linked with England
through the Marriage of The Thistle and The
Rose, it seemed that the country could look for-
ward to a period of peace and so the Hamiltons
abandoned living in the draughty old peel tower at
Kinneil, which they had required for safety in the
more turbulent, strife-torn times, in favour of the
greater comforts of a new modern L shaped man-

sion which they built on an adjacent site. The peace, however, was short lived because James IV in support of his old allies the French soon went to war with his English in-laws and in 1513 paid the price when he and all his young Scottish nobles, the famous Flowers of the Forest, were slaughtered on Flodden's bloody field.

The King was succeeded by his infant son James V, and Hamilton, Earl of Arran, found himself at the centre of the resultant turmoil when he was appointed Regent of Scotland and had to fight off the rival Douglas claim for supremacy over the young monarch.

Just as with the royal family, when Hamilton died in 1529 he was succeeded by his son while he was still a minor. The boy was placed under the guardianship of his uncle and under his guidance began the construction of Hamilton Palace.

Chapter three:

Bid for the Throne

It was indeed fitting that young Hamilton, second Earl of Arran, had a palace as his home because he was a very important young gentleman. Indeed as great grandson of King James II, following the death of James V after the Battle of Solway Moss in 1542, he was no less than heir presumptive to the Scottish throne. As such he was appointed regent to the little week-old Mary, Queen of Scots, when she came to the throne in December of that year.

While she was a babe in arms, the campaign to use the infant Mary to strengthen Scottish links with other countries began. To begin with Hamilton backed the English bid and in the following year, 1543, signed the Treaty of Greenwich which promised that when of age Mary would marry the then six-year-old Edward, Prince of Wales, thus repeating the process started forty years earlier by the Marriage of The Thistle and The Rose.

This did not meet the wishes of the young Queen's mother, Mary of Guise or of her chief adviser Cardinal Beaton, who both wanted an alliance with Catholic France. Within a year Hamilton was persuaded to change his mind and to renege on the Treaty of Greenwich, thus causing Edward's father Henry III to engage in the famous 'Rough Wooing' invasion of the Scottish Borders.

Instead, Regent Hamilton now fell in line with the Queen Mother and the Cardinal to marry Mary to the Dauphin, Francis, Crown Prince of France. It is suggested that perhaps Hamilton's change of mind was influenced by questions which were being asked about his father's second marriage of which he was a product and thus his own legitimacy and that, as the Roman Catholic Church was the deciding factor in such cases, he had to ensure its support. In any case, Hamilton was richly rewarded for his change of support, because Mary of Guise ensured that he was granted the French Dukedom of Chateauherault.

Five years later, in 1554, Hamilton threw

in his lot further with the Queen Mother by agreeing to surrender his position as Regent in her favour, in return for her promise that if Mary, Queen of Scots should fail to produce a child, then he should become King of Scotland.

Hamilton's hopes of possibly becoming the Scottish monarch suffered a severe setback in 1558 when, following her marriage to Francis, Mary agreed that he also should become King of Scots.

His chances rose again soon afterwards when the Protestant Lords of the Congregation approached them in secret to become their candidate for the throne if they succeeded in deposing the Catholic Queen. The one problem for Hamilton was that his heir was at the time held prisoner in France where he had been leader of the Scots Guard, but as soon as young James escaped, he agreed to champion the Protestant cause.

Then in 1560 events overtook Hamilton yet again when the unexpected and very untimely death of the Dauphin resulted in the widowed Mary's return to Scotland. Hamilton decided that the best hope of securing the Scottish throne for his family was to propose that his heir James would be the ideal second husband for the Queen. Instead, Mary announced her betrothal to her cousin Henry, Lord Darnley. Furious at the threat which this match posed to the Hamiltons becoming the future royal family, the Duke, as he was popularly known in Scotland on account of his French title, raised an armed uprising against the Queen. Despite support for the Earl of Moray, he was defeated and forced to seek refuge in France, where he resided in great style at Chateauherault, until after Mary's third marriage to Lord Bothwell and her subsequently being deposed from the Scottish throne.

Sadly by this time Hamilton's heir James, Third Earl of Arran, who had always been a somewhat erratic young man, had now become completely mad, so Hamilton again changed sides and decided to return to Scotland to support the Queen's cause during her exile in England. This did much damage to his family's cause and in 1569 Hamilton himself was even imprisoned by his former ally, the Earl of Moray. Three years later in 1572 the by then elderly Hamilton gave in and was persuaded by the English to sign the Pacification of Perth which recognised Mary Queen of Scots' son James as her successor.

Thus ended the Hamilton's hopes as the country's premier noble family of wresting the Scottish throne from the royal house of Stewart.

Mary was no friend to the Hamiltons

Chapter four:

A formidable woman and ghostly lady

The Hamiltons supported the royalist side in the Civil Wars of the 1640's, so Oliver Cromwell had no compunction about commandeering Kinneil House when he invaded Scotland in 1650.

Kinneil was put at the disposal of his commander General Monk. He in turn gave it as his residence to his subordinate, General Lilbourne. As the posting to Scotland looked like being a long one, the General decided to bring his young wife, Lady Alice, whom he had only recently married, to take up residence with him at Kinneil.

Sadly the marriage of Lord and Lady Lilbourne did not turn out to be a happy one. The beautiful lady Alice was very homesick and there were frequent rows and quarrels between her and her husband. Lord Lilbourne in the end decided to teach his disobedient young wife a salutary lesson by ordering that she should be locked up in a small attic room high on the west side of the old peel tower at Kinneil.

Lady Lilbourne was, however, not to be so easily subdued and late one night, under cover of darkness, she managed to escape from her tiny turret prison. Without a sound she slipped down the steep, stone-flagged spiral stairs and out of the house. Wearing only a flimsy white nightgown, she dashed along the pitch-black, tree-lined drive towards the lights of the long, low rows of cottages where the miners, who worked in the Hamilton family coal pits, lived at Castleloan. Just as she was almost within reach of the safety of the houses, she heard the noise of her husband and servants and dogs coming in search for her.

Swiftly she sought some place to hide. The baying of the hounds and the sounds of her pursuers grew even nearer. Just as they were almost upon her, she suddenly spotted a hollow tree. Desperately she clambered up and into the hollow bough. With a feeling of relief, she heard the clamour of her husband and his followers as they rushed by. From the distance she heard her husband and the servants hammering on the doors of the miners' rows. Angrily, they barged in and searched the little houses, but, of course, to no avail.

She heard her furious husband and the servants noisily making their way back to Kinneil. It looked as if she had evaded them. Just as they passed the hollow tree, however, Lord Lilbourne glanced up. Amongst the leaves he spotted a flash of white. It was a wisp of her white nightgown. Lady Lilbourne was seized and, as the howling of the hounds shattered the silence of the black night, was hauled brutally back to the big house.

Lady Alice still refused to give in to her husband. Again he ordered that she be imprisoned in the room high in the old peel tower. Now Lady Lilbourne resorted to the only way of escape which she knew would free her from her soldier husband's cruelty. She threw herself from the narrow window. Down, down, down she plunged. Almost two hundred feet below, she crashed to her death on the rock-covered bed of the Gil Burn.

The tragic suicide of Lady Lilbourne did not, however, end her connection with the Hamilton's home. Ever since, the ghostly apparition of the White Lady as she became known, because of the tell-tale diaphanous nightwear which caused her capture and death, has returned to haunt old Kinneil. Her eerie wails, screams and shrieks are said to echo through its now ruined and roofless corridors and halls on dark windy nights, when gales blow up the nearby River Forth. Even by day she is not forgotten, because, when local children visit Kinneil on holiday trips or school project outings, they never miss the opportunity to chant and skip to the three hundred year old rhyme.

"Poor Lady Lilbourne, died in the Gil Burn."

The occupation of Hamilton estates by Cromwell's supporters meant that their financial affairs were in dire straits by the time Anne, or Anna as she was often known, daughter of James and niece of William, succeeded William in 1651 and became Duchess in her own right. The new Duchess Anna, however, proved far more able than any of the Hamilton men when it came to putting the family's fortunes to rights.

In April, 1657, Anna married William, the eldest son of the first Marquis of Douglas, thus introducing the Douglas name which from then on became so associated with that of Hamilton. Together they set about managing the Hamilton estates and especially their coal pits and salt pans. They were assisted in re-establishing the family's place in Scottish society by the Restoration to the throne of King Charles II in 1660 and soon found royal favour.

In September, 1660, the King bestowed upon Douglas the titles of Duke of Hamilton, Marquis of Clydeside, Earl of Arran, Lanark and Selkirk and a year later the Duchess received from the King a regent of the lands and baronies of Hamilton, Kinneil and all of the family's other Scottish possessions, including those on the Isle of Arran.

Duchess Anna used her favour with the King to persuade him to grant burgh status to Borrowstounness, the Burgh Town on the Ness or the nose of land and Bo'ness as it was soon known became the harbour for the export of all the Kinneil estate's cargoes of coal and salt. The charter creating Bo'ness a burgh also gave the town the right to hold an annual fair which it is still famous for doing to this day.

While to begin with the Hamiltons had supported the Restoration of the Stewarts to the throne, in the 1680's they changed sides and at the Bloodless Revolution of 1688 were amongst the first to welcome the coming of William of Orange.

On the other hand their eldest son and heir, James, as befitted his name, remained a staunch Jacobite. In the 1690's he played a leading role in Scottish politics, forming a party to support the colonisation of Darien. Three of the ships for the Darien expedition were built in Bo'ness and when they set sail carried with them the hopes of the country. The venture was, however, a disastrous failure, leaving Scotland almost bankrupt and the way was open for the Union of the Parliaments with England in 1707.

At first Hamilton opposed the Union, but at the last moment, prevailed upon by his kinswoman Queen Anne, lent his support, an act for which many Scots never forgave him.

In 1941, Hitler's deputy, Rudolph Hess, flew to Scotland to meet Alfred Douglas, the 13th Duke of Hamilton, in the belief that he was sufficiently powerful to intervene with Winston Churchill to end the hostilities. Whether that meeting could have in any way changed the course of the war will never be known because, after parachuting onto the fields of a farm near Eaglesham, not far from Hamilton, Hess was arrested before he could make contact with the Duke, tried for war crimes and held in solitary confinement in prison until he ended his own life.

Hess certainly would not have found the Duke in residence at Hamilton Palace because the great house had been demolished in the 1920's, when it was found to be dangerously undermined by the family's own coal workings. Built a century before in 1828, by the architect David Hamilton, the house was in its time one of the finest stately homes in Britain with a classical facade over 250 feet in length.

Hamilton Palace stood just to the south of the family's chapel and mausoleum, whose distinctive domed roof is still a familiar landmark to travellers on the M74, Glasgow to Carlisle motorway. It is not open to the public, but a little further to the south Chateauherault Country Park, formed from the grounds of the former palace, welcomes visitors.